Song Lyrics by Anna B. Warner
Illustrated by Nancy Carter & Terry Julien

ISBN 978-1-4964-0315-5

Printed in China

21	20	19	18	17	16
7	6	5	4	3	2

Tyndale House Publishers, Inc.
Carol Stream, Illinois

Jesus loves me, this I know

For the Bible tells me so.

Little ones to him belong,

They are weak,

But he is strong.

Yes, Jesus loves me!
Yes, Jesus loves me!

Yes, Jesus loves me!
The Bible tells me so.

I love Jesus and I know

He wants me his love to show

By the way I live each day—

In my home, at school, at play!

Yes, I love Jesus!
Yes, I love Jesus!

Yes, I love Jesus!
My life will tell him so.

Nothing in the whole world can separate us from the love of God that is in Jesus. —*from Romans 8:39*

Let's Talk about It

1. Where does it say that Jesus loves you?

2. Who belongs to Jesus?

3. What does Jesus want you to do?

4. Where can you show love?

5. Do you love Jesus?

Matching Items

Jesus

blocks

cat

truck

Word Search

L J F J V X E L

M E R E W T O P

X S U S B V E H

X S C U E L O K

I R X S B M I V

K E D I E W J H

Z V B G R B G D

Q P O R T G U R

Find these words

BIBLE • **HOME** • **JESUS** • **LOVE**

Craft Activity

Make a flower basket and share Jesus' love with a friend!

Things you will need:

- paper or Styrofoam cup
- markers
- string or yarn
- scissors
- flowers

What to do:

1. Use the markers to decorate the cup.

2. Ask an adult to poke a hole in either side of the cup near the edges.

3. String a piece of yarn through the holes. Have an adult help you tie a knot at each end to make a handle.

4. Fill the cup with pretty flowers.

5. Hang the cup of flowers on a friend's or neighbor's door to make them smile.

COLORING PAGE

COLORING PAGE

Shape a lifestyle of faith expression in your child

— Our passion is to provide a creative outlet for kids to express their faith in a fun and meaningful way. Cultivate a deeper connection as you teach your child about the impact of God's love, building a legacy of relationship, creativity, and faith to last a lifetime.

Using interactive games, puzzles, and other activities, **Faith That Sticks resources** are a great go-to place for parents who want to teach their kids to love God and to know how much he loves them!

learn more at faiththatsticks.com

More about Reading Levels

PRE-READERS

Books appropriate for pre-readers have

- pictures that reinforce the text
- simple words
- short, simple sentences
- repetition of words and patterns
- large print

BEGINNING READERS

Books appropriate for beginning readers have

- pictures that reinforce the text
- intermediate words
- longer sentences
- simple stories
- dialogue between story characters

INDEPENDENT READERS

Books appropriate for independent readers have

- less need for pictorial support with the text
- more advanced vocabulary
- paragraphs
- longer stories
- more complex subjects

" There are perhaps no days of our childhood we lived so fully as those we spent with a favorite book." — MARCEL PROUST